this book belongs to:

_____

For my Jidoor (grandpa), Mohammed Israili.

مكرس لجدي محمد إسرائيل

On a warm Australian morning when the golden glow of the sun beamed across the green grass, Milo, the big brindle dog, went for a walk.

As he walked, the birds sang from the gum trees, and the busy bees danced amongst the sweetly scented pollen.

Despite having few friends, Milo loved his walks. But he wished he could share them with a friend.

Other dogs were scared of Milo because of his size, and would quickly scurry to the other side of the street when they saw him coming.

Little did they know, Milo's big size came with an even bigger heart, filled with love for everyone and anyone.

Milo then noticed something strange...

There, alone and with an injured wing, was a little pink Galah named Cracker.

At first, Cracker was scared of Milo because they were so different.

Dogs, especially big ones like Milo, are not usually friendly to birds.
But Milo was different, he wanted to protect Cracker and keep him safe.

Cracker had feathers and Milo had fur.

Cracker was pink and Milo was brown.

Cracker was small and Milo was big.

Cracker squawked and Milo barked.

Although they were very different, they both had one thing in common.

They needed a friend.

Milo would sit near Cracker and keep him company.

Refusing to leave his side.

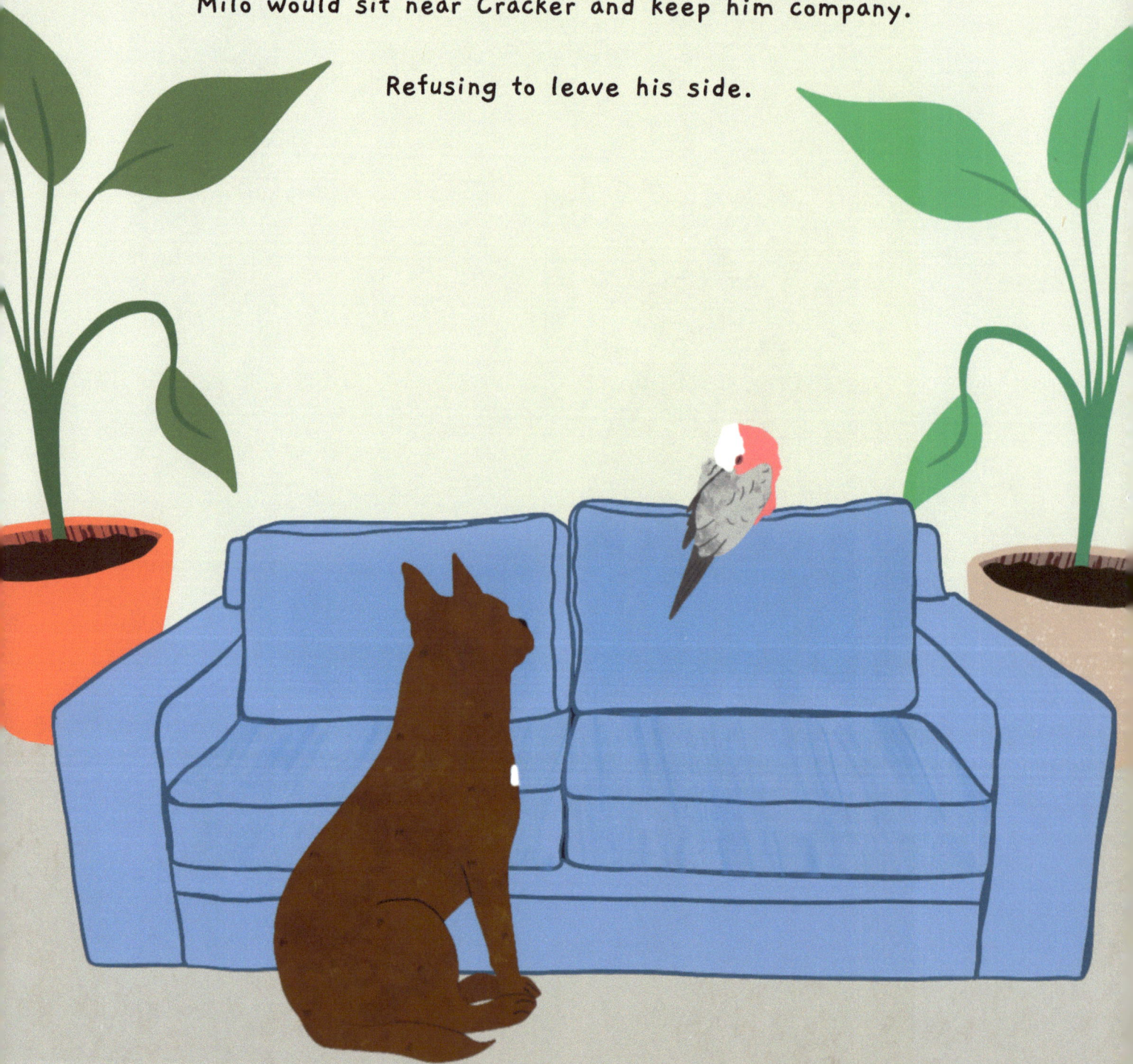

While Cracker's wing grew stronger,
so did his friendship with Milo.

They would do everything together...

They played together.

They ate together.

They napped together.

ZZzz

ZZzz

They laughed together.

They became best friends.

Then one night when the air was cold and crisp,
Cracker got a fright and flew away...

He was lost and all alone, again.

Milo would sit and wait all day for weeks...
just hoping his feathered friend would come back.

But Milo could not wait any longer.
With a determined heart, he set off on a journey to find Cracker.

He looked over at the shrubs and saw five rainbow lorikeets dynamically dancing.

But Cracker was not over there.

He looked in the bottle brush trees and saw four cockatoos proudly playing.

But Cracker was not in there.

He looked down at the grass and saw three magpies fiercely foraging.

But Cracker was not down there.

HA! HA! HA!

He looked up in the gum trees and saw two Kookaburras laughing loudly.

But Cracker was not up there, either.

Milo searched, here, there and everywhere.
He even searched night,

and day, refusing to give up.

Then as Milo was walking home...

He noticed one pink Galah sitting sadly amongst the yellow flowers of a wattle tree.

They squawked and barked with happiness!

Cracker and Milo were so happy to finally be together, again.

As the sun set, painting the sky purple and orange, Milo walked home with his tail wagging and his best friend, Cracker the Galah, by his side.

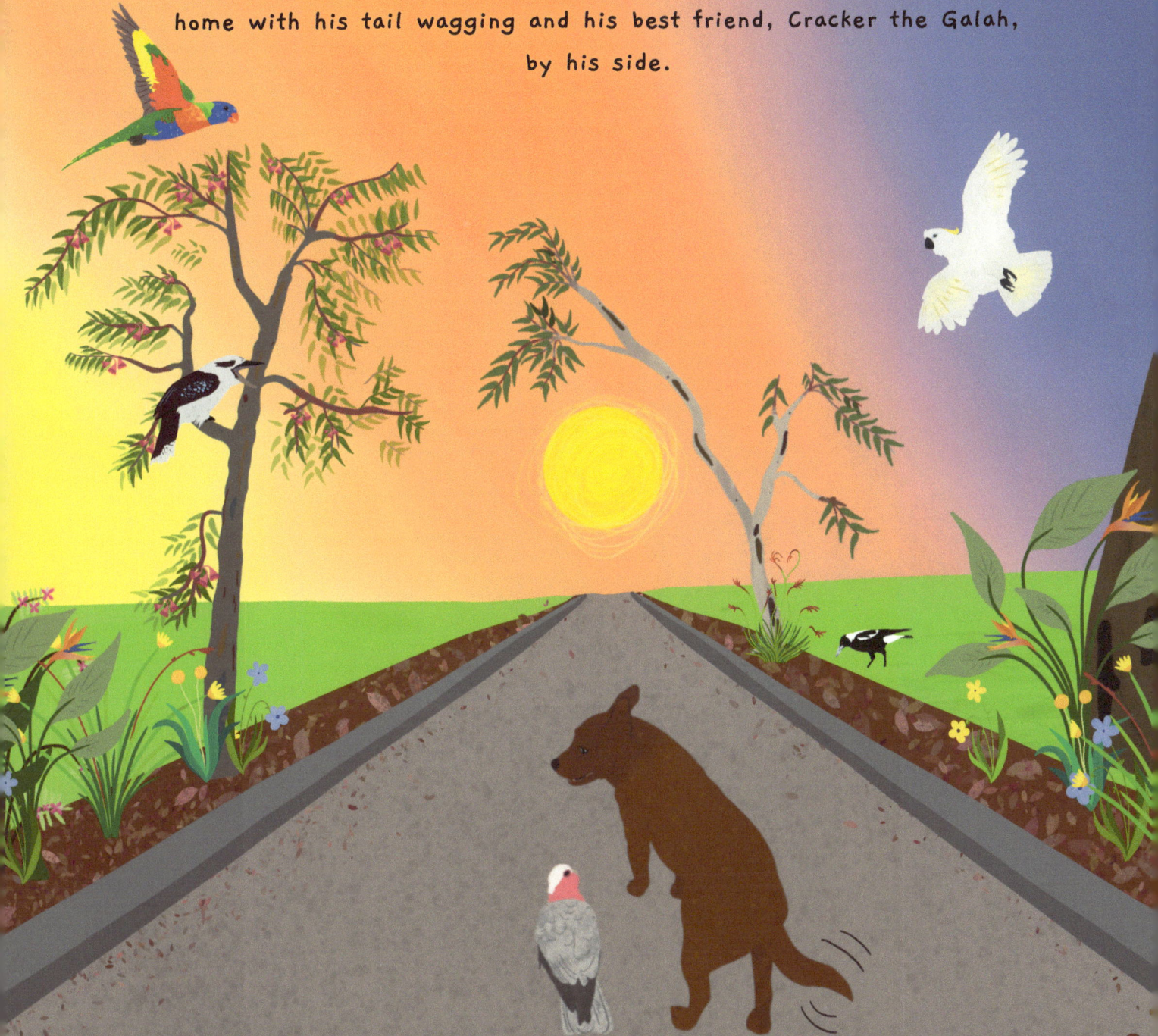

Although they were a different size, a different colour, and a different species, their love for each other was all that mattered.

Where you find one, you'll find the other.
Side by side, feathers to fur, paw to claw.

Based on the true story of Cracker & Milo.

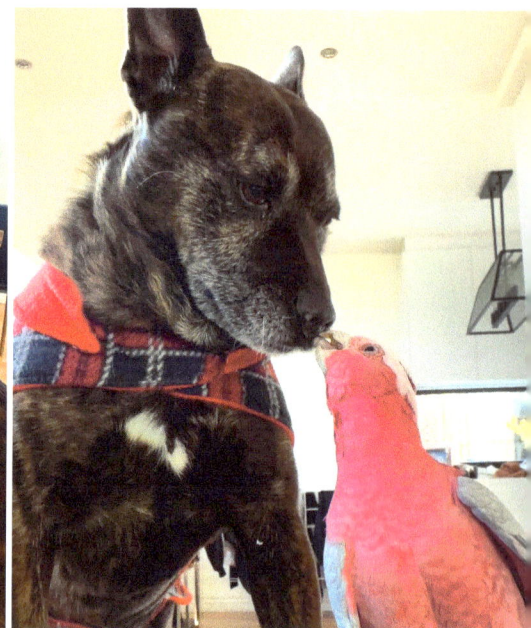

To see more, follow them on Instagram & TikTok @crackerandmilo

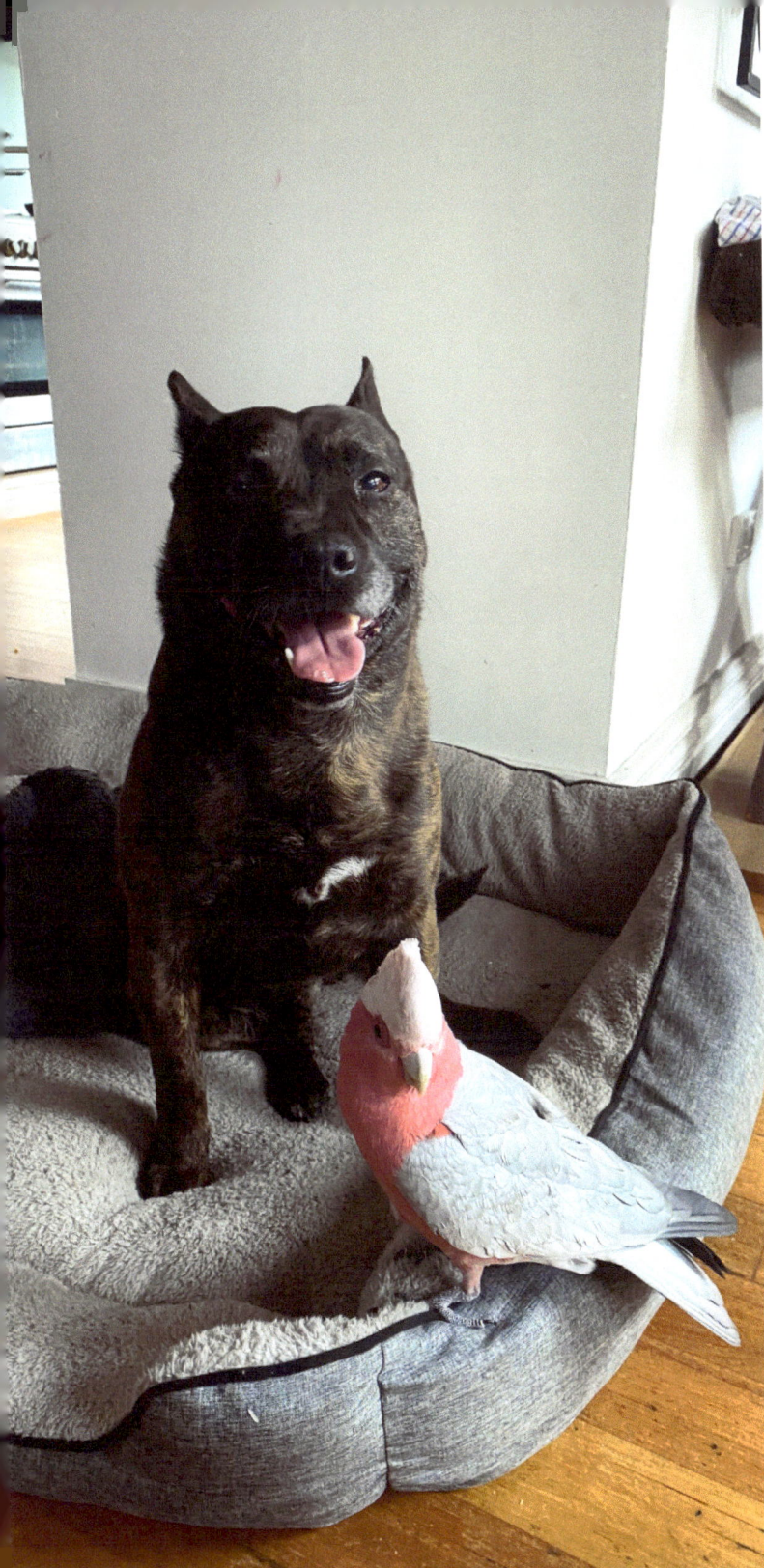

This picture was taken on the day we found Cracker and brought him home, three weeks after he went missing.

Milo was so happy he was smiling from ear to ear for hours.

www.ingramcontent.com/pod-product-compliance
Lightning Source LLC
Chambersburg PA
CBHW042009090426
42811CB00015B/1592

9780646893495